GARDENING
WITH
God

LESSONS
FROM THE
MASTER GARDENER

Anita
Wadley Schlaht

Doodle and Peck Publishing
Yukon, Oklahoma

©2023 Anita Wadley Schlaht

ISBN: 979-8-9866380-1-0 (paperback)
ISBN: 979-8-9866380-2-7 (hardcover)

Doodle and Peck Publishing
413 Cedarburg Ct
Yukon, OK 73099
405.354.7422
www.doodleandpeck.com

RELIGION / Biblical Studies / Bible Study Guides
RELIGION / Biblical Meditations / General
RELIGION / Biblical Studies / General

Library of Congress Control Number: 2023930965

She taught me about God and the garden. I can still hear her singing "In the Garden," one of her favorite hymns.

Anita Wadley Schlaht

"I come to the garden alone, while the dew is still on the roses;
And the voice I hear, falling on my ear, the Son of God discloses.

And He walks with me, and He talks with me,
And He tells me I am His own;
And the joy we share as we tarry there
None other has ever known.

He speaks, and the sound of His voice is so sweet the birds hush their singing;
And the melody that He gave to me within my heart is ringing.

And He walks with me, and He talks with me,
And He tells me I am His own;
And the joy we share as we tarry there
None other has ever known.

Text and Music by C. Austin Miles

TABLE OF CONTENTS

TABLE OF CONTENTS, continued

GARDENING INSTRUCTIONS

*"The Lord will guide you always; he will satisfy your needs
in a sun-scorched land and will strengthen your frame.
You will be like a well-watered garden, like
a spring whose waters never fail." ISAIAH 58:11 (NIV)*

In September 1999, I embarked upon an adventure to clear the back half of the one acre lot on which our new home was being built. Having experienced the "bulldozer effect" in the front and losing many small, native, flowering trees, I was determined to carefully clear and trim the back of the property myself. While working outside in the cool fall air, God's Word, as it relates to gardening and nature, came to life. Over and over references to trees, vines, well-watered gardens, grass, flowers, thorns, etc., touched my heart and showed me that He is the Master Gardener. I was determined to write down and remember the lessons He taught me so that I could share them with others.

However, during this process, "weeds" hindered my path. Procrastination, busyness, and discouragement often kept me from the task. I pray, now that these pages are completed, God will use them, to speak to you. May God's Word give you all the "gardening instructions" needed for your life.

Listen closely. Do you hear Him calling you out to the garden?

Dig a little deeper:

"The Spirit of the Sovereign Lord is on me, because the Lord has anointed me to preach good news to the poor. He has sent me to bind up the brokenhearted, to proclaim freedom for the captives and release from darkness for the prisoners, to proclaim the year of the Lord's favor and the day of vengeance of our God, to comfort all who mourn, to provide for those who grieve in Zion—to bestow on them a crown of beauty instead of ashes, the oil of gladness instead of mourning, and a garment of praise instead of a spirit of despair. They will be called oaks of righteousness, a planting of the Lord, for the display of His splendor."

ISAIAH 61:1-3 (NIV)

Prayer:

God, begin today to make me into an oak of Your righteousness for the display of Your splendor. In Jesus' name, Amen.

Notes:
_____
_____
_____
_____
_____
_____
_____
_____
_____
_____

THE ROSE BUSH

"A voice is calling, clear the way for the Lord in the wilderness; make smooth in the desert a highway for our God. Let every valley be lifted up, and every mountain and hill be made low; and let the rough ground become a plain, and the rugged terrain a broad valley. Then the glory of the Lord will be revealed, and all flesh will see it together; for the mouth of the Lord has spoken." A voice says, "Call out." Then He answered, "What shall I call out?" All flesh is grass, and all its loveliness is like the flower of the field. The grass withers, the flower fades, when the breath of the Lord blows upon it; surely the people are grass. The grass withers, the flower fades, but the word of our God stands forever." Isaiah 40:3-8 (NAS)

The first day on the job I decided to attack a clump of oak trees on the corner of the back yard, close to the house. Using an axe, I chopped down small sapling trees and vines from around the base. As I cleared away the brush I was amazed to discover a rose bush. Years ago when the trees were much smaller, someone had intentionally planted it there. As time passed it had been neglected and weeds had grown up and hidden it from view.

Your life may be like that rose bush. As Christians, the Holy Spirit is in our hearts. However, our days often get crowded with the busy stuff of living and sadly, sometimes even sin. These weeds grow up and hide Him.

But when we chop away the weeds of "busy-ness", confess any hidden sins, and remove them from our lives, the beauty of Jesus Christ can once again be revealed.

As soon as I cut the weeds away from the sickly little rose, more sunlight reached it. In just a few days it put on new leaves and began to thrive. By spring, the lovely rose bush was healthy with the promise of flowers to come.

As Christians, we are meant to bloom and shine too. When there's plenty of room in our life for the Son, we are able to grow and bring joy to those around us, just as our Heavenly Father, the Master Gardener, planned.

Are there any weeds you need to clear away in your life?
Do you think you are getting enough of the Son today?

Dig a little deeper:

"Sow your seed in the morning, and do not be idle in the evening, for you do not know whether morning or evening sowing will succeed, or whether both of them alike will be good. The light is pleasant, and it is good for the eyes to see the sun." Ecclesiastes 11:6-7 (NAS)

Prayer:

God, begin today to make me into an oak of Your righteousness for the display of Your splendor. In Jesus' name, Amen.

Notes: _____

DAY 3

A GOD OF ORDER

"For God is not a God of disorder but of peace."
1 Corinthians 14:33 (NIV)

When we purchased the property the back yard was covered with a mass of vines, leaves, dead branches, and wildflowers. Everywhere wild plum saplings competed for space and sunlight. Looking at an area, I would imagine what I wanted it to look like. Then, one stem at a time, I decided what to cut or pull out and what to leave. My goal was order, shape and symmetry.

The remaining plants were pruned and shaped so they would grow stronger and straighter. I tried to leave all of them, but eventually cut some of them out. This resulted in stronger, straighter trees that complemented the landscape, instead of crowding it.

The temptation to get ahead of myself and jump from one area to the other was always a struggle. However, I discovered that I got better results if I worked diligently in a smaller area before moving on. The work was hard and many times I worked all day. As I turned to leave, I would look back at the results and sometimes I would see great progress; other days it was barely obvious I had even been there.

On the days when little progress was made, glancing back over an area I had cleared before, I was satisfied and encouraged to see what was possible, and it gave me the hope, courage, and strength to continue.

When God created the world He created order, not confusion. Jesus' life, a life of order and purpose, gives us a picture of what our lives can be. I must allow God to prune some of the things from my life so that I can grow stronger and straighter, submitting to His master plan. Sometimes it is hard to see and understand what He is doing and how He is working. But when I remember what He has done in the past, I'm confident in placing my trust in Him.

How does God want to bring order to your life?
How is Satan using confusion to divert you from godly goals?

Dig a little deeper:

"For I am confident of this very thing, that He who began a good work in you will perfect it until the day of Christ Jesus." Philippians 1:6 (NAS)

"For even though I am absent in body, nevertheless I am with you in spirit, rejoicing to see your good discipline and the stability of your faith in Christ." Colossians 2:5 (NAS)

Prayer:

God, help me to be focused on the tasks You have given me. As I see Your faithful hand in the past, help me to trust You to give wisdom and order to the future. In Jesus' name, Amen.

Notes: _____

GOD'S UNIQUE GARDEN

"The mind of man plans his way, but the Lord directs his steps."
Proverbs 16:9 (NIV)

Letting the wildflowers and wild plants survive in our yard was fascinating to watch. Through the months there was almost always something in bloom. White, pink, purple and yellow wildflowers popped up everywhere. Different types of grasses grew tall with fuzzy tops; all shapes of leaves turned yellow, orange and red when fall came. Some trees lost their leaves and some stayed green through the winter.

I learned quickly that…

• Each plant is special and unique. In its own way each grows, buds, blossoms, bears seed, and then withers away.

• Each plant has a special place where it grows best; some grow in the shade, others need more sun.

• Each plant has a purpose. Some are just pretty to look at while others provide food for the animals in the area. Dead plants and leaves become compost that feeds the roots and seeds for the next year.

Just like the plants, each one of us is a unique creation of God. He says to Jeremiah, "Before I formed you in the womb I knew you." (Jeremiah 1:5a)You are not an accident. Your interests, abilities, and talents are a gift from God. They are meant to be used for His purposes.

Do you feel special and unique to God right now? Why or why not? Are you letting your light shine for His purpose?

Dig a little deeper:

"You are the light of the world. A city, set on a hill cannot be hidden. Nor do men light a lamp, and put it under a basket, but on the lampstand; and it gives light to all who are in the house. Let your light shine before men in such a way that they may see your good works, and glorify your Father who is in heaven." Matthew 5:14-16 (NIV)

Prayer:

Prayer: Thank you for making me unique and loving me just as I am. Help me to shine for You today. In Jesus' name, Amen.

Notes: _____

_____

_____

_____

_____

_____

_____

_____

_____

_____

DAY
5

BEGINNINGS

"Then God said, 'Let the earth sprout vegetation, plants yielding seed, and fruit trees bearing fruit after their kind, with seed in them, on the earth; and it was so. And the earth brought forth vegetation, plants yielding seed after their kind, and trees bearing fruit, with seed in them, after their kind; and God saw that it was good." Genesis 1:11-12 (NAS)

Isn't it interesting that the story of mankind begins in a garden? The Master Gardener created mankind in the garden, for the garden. God created this beautiful garden, Eden, for Adam and Eve, his creation. He provided everything they needed, and only asked one thing in return--obedience.

Man's rebellion against God also began in that garden. Satan used a tree that was beautiful and desirable to tempt Adam and Eve. They chose to disobey God, which cost them their home in the garden. And ultimately, their rebellion cost God his only Son, Jesus Christ.

God loved us so much, though, He couldn't bear to be separated from his creation for eternity. So He sent Jesus to pay the penalty for our sin. Everyone who accepts God's gift of salvation begins a new life, and will live with Him forever, in a paradise even better than that first perfect garden he created.

If you died today, do you know for certain that you would go to heaven? If not, today you can have a new beginning by trusting Jesus as your personal Savior and Lord.

What is keeping you from being obedient to God?

Dig a little deeper:

"And the Lord God planted a garden toward the east, in Eden; and there He placed the man whom He had formed. And out of the ground the Lord God caused to grow every tree that is pleasing to the sight and good for food; the tree of life also in the midst of the garden, and the tree of the knowledge of good and evil." Genesis 2:8-9 (NAS)

"Then the Lord God took the man and put him into the garden of Eden to cultivate it and keep it. And the Lord God commanded the man, saying, 'From any tree of the garden you may eat freely; but from the tree of the knowledge of good and evil you shall not eat, for in the day that you eat from it you shall surely die.' Then the Lord God said, 'It is not good for the man to be alone; I will make him a helper suitable for him.' And the Lord God fashioned into a woman the rib which He had taken from the man, and brought her to the man." Genesis 2:15-18, 22 (NAS)

Prayer:

God, forgive me for my disobedience. Thank you for sending Jesus to die for me so that someday I can make my home with you in heaven. In Jesus' name, Amen.

Notes:

DAY 6

"DE-VINE PROTECTION

Finally, be strong in the Lord and in his mighty power. Put on the full armor of God so that you can take your stand against the devil's schemes. For our struggle is not against flesh and blood, but against the rulers, against the authorities, against the powers of this dark world and against the spiritual forces of evil in the heavenly realms. Therefore, put on the full armor of God, so that when the day of evil comes, you may be able to stand your ground, and after you have done everything, to stand.
Ephesians 6:10-13 (NIV)

As I began to clear around the base of the trees, I encountered many vicious, thorny vines. Mingled in were wild blackberry bushes that dotted the back one-half of our acre lot. These long, spiny runners slashed my hands and arms as I worked to clear them away completely from some areas, and tame and contain them in others. I either had to wear long-sleeved shirts and suffer from the heat, or be more comfortable in short sleeves and gloves, but have the thorns rip my skin. Many days I came away bloody and sore.

The first lesson God taught me as I thinned the blackberries was that thorny vines hurt, and it's important to wear protective gear when you go out to do battle with them. He reminded me of all the times I had gone into the battle of life unprotected and had come away bloody and sore. The Bible tells us to put on the "full armor of God" before we go out to fight the enemy. Sometimes we feel that the armor is restrictive and uncomfortable, as were my long-sleeved shirts. But we need God's protection—the sword of the Spirit, the shield of faith, the breastplate of righteousness, and the helmet of salvation. And we need to be prepared with the gospel of peace. We need to wrap ourselves in the truth of God's Word and understand who our fight is against. Satan's fiery darts, like blackberry thorns, are sharp and can injure us if we are unprotected.

Are you bloody and sore from doing battle without the proper protection?
Is God's armor too restrictive for your life?
Can you think of a time when God protected you from the enemy?

Dig a little deeper:

I will rejoice greatly in the Lord, my soul will exult in my God; for He has clothed me with garments of salvation, he has wrapped me with a robe of righteousness, as a bridegroom decks himself with a garland, and as a bride adorns herself with her jewels. For as the earth brings forth its sprouts, and as a garden causes the things sown in it to spring up, so the Lord God will cause righteousness and praise to spring up before all the nations. Isaiah 61:10-11 (NAS)

Prayer:

Prayer: God, remind me each day not to go into battle unprepared. Teach me to be protected by hiding Your Word in my heart. In Jesus' name, Amen.

Notes:

UNDERGROUND CONNECTIONS

"Remain in me, and I will remain in you. No branch can bear fruit by itself; it must remain in the vine. Neither can you bear fruit unless you remain in me." John 15:5 (NIV)

For years the blackberry bushes had grown wild and spread, forming huge impenetrable thickets. As I began to clear out the vines, I noticed they were all connected underground. As I would pull out one it connected to another. The plants had multiplied, popping up everywhere, literally taking over.

When the new plants first come up they have tiny thorns that are only slightly sharp and only a bit uncomfortable to pull out. But the longer they are left to grow and develop, the sharper and more painful the thorns become. Especially on the old, dried, deadwood stalks.

Sin can be like an underground blackberry vine. If neglected, it will take over our lives, growing and spreading.

God wants us to pull out those roots of sin before they have time to grow and become thorny monsters. He wants us to "not let the sun go down while we are still angry" (Ephesians 4:26) but deal with our disagreements and confess our sins to each other. If we ask Him to remove those hidden sins, the Master Gardener will prune the thorns, runners, and deadwood before they take hold and spread.

There is one positive thing about the spreading blackberry vines, however: this is where the blooms and berries form. This is where the fruit is, on the new growth. The Bible says that He is the vine and we are the branches. Staying connected to Him and to other believers gives us the strength to root out the sin that creeps in and allow new growth to happen.

Is there unconfessed sin that keeps popping up in your life?
Have you asked the Master Gardener to help you dig it out and deal with it?

Dig a little deeper:

"Let us hold fast the confession of our hope without wavering, for He who promised is faithful; and let us consider how to stimulate one another to love and good deeds, not forsaking our own assembling together, as is the habit of some, but encouraging one another; and all the more, as you see the day drawing near." Hebrews 10:23-25 (NAS)

Prayer:

Heavenly Father, reveal to me my deep-rooted sins. Help me to pull them out with your strength and stay connected to You, the true vine. Bring others into my life who desire to grow in the knowledge of You. In Jesus' name, Amen.

Notes: _____

DAY
8

THE FRUIT OF THE VINE

"I am the true vine, and my Father is the gardener. He cuts off every branch in me that bears no fruit, while every branch that does bear fruit he prunes so that it will be even more fruitful. I am the vine; you are the branches. If a man remains in me and I in him, he will bear much fruit; apart from me you can do nothing. If anyone does not remain in me, he is like a branch that is thrown away and withers; such branches are picked up, thrown into the fire and burned. If you remain in me and my words remain in you, ask whatever you wish, and it will be given you. This is to my Father's glory, that you bear much fruit, showing yourselves to be my disciples. As the Father has loved me, so have I loved you. Now remain in my love. If you obey my commands, you will remain in my love, just as I have obeyed my Father's commands and remain in his love. I have told you this so that my joy may be in you and that your joy may be complete. My command is this: Love each other as I have loved you. Greater love has no one than this that he lay down his life for his friends. You are my friends if you do what I command." John 15:1-3, 6-14 (NIV)

Good vines are the ones that produce fruit. There are two kinds of good vines that I encountered in my days of work–blackberry vines and grape vines. Grape vines are pretty and add texture to the landscape. They tend to grow along the ground and not up into the trees. They do not strangle the trees like the Virginia Creeper or thorny vines. I have yet to see any grapes produced on them, however. Maybe they are just for show and aren't true grapevines. The other good vines are the blackberries. Although painful to work with and difficult to train, they produce lovely little white flowers and the berries I love to eat.

There are at least two kinds of Christians. Those that produce fruit and those that do not. Some Christians are content to just grow horizontally, never getting any closer to the Son, never producing fruit.

But, Jesus is the true Vine and we are the branches. If we stay connected to Jesus, the Vine, we will live productive lives. If we spend time daily with Him in prayer, Bible Study, and meditation we will grow more like Him and produce the fruit of His Spirit living in us: "love, joy, peace, patience, kindness, goodness, faithfulness, gentleness, and self-control." (Galatians 5:22)

Are you connected to the true Vine?
Are you producing good "fruit"?
Do you desire to grow toward the Son instead of clinging close to the things of this world?

Dig a little deeper:

"This is to my Father's glory, that you bear much fruit, showing yourselves to be my disciples." (John 15:8)

Prayer:

Jesus, thank you for your love for me. Help me to remain in your love and bear much fruit. In Your name, Amen.

Notes:

GARDENING TOOLS

"Consider it all joy, my brethren, when we encounter various trials; knowing that the testing of our faith produces endurance. And let endurance have its perfect result, that we may be perfect and complete, lacking in nothing. But if any of you lacks wisdom, let him ask of God, who gives to all men generously and without reproach, and it will be given to him." James 1:2-5 (NAS)

It took many different tools to finally clear the overgrown blackberries so the ground was ready for planting grass. I shopped the garden store to find better tools to do the job. I had to invest the time to search for these tools and make them a part of my toolbox.

And so it is with our lives. When we allow the Spirit to teach us and give us the tools we need, we can clear away the thorns and become fertile soil for God's future plantings. These tools don't just rain down from heaven. God has already given us His Word. It is up to us to find and hone our tools and gifts through prayer and study.

While clearing out the tough vines, I found that power tools were the most effective. Often, my strength alone was not enough to cut through the dry, woody stalks. But when I used my power brush cutter, it sliced through those vines like butter.

How many times have I tried to do God's work in my own strength? God says that apart from Him I can do nothing. I must keep my tools sharp and in working order. And I must stay "connected to the Vine" drawing on the power of the Holy Spirit.

How are your tools working?
Do they need to be sharpened by the Master Gardener?
Do you need to search God's word for better tools?
Or do you need to connect to the True Vine to receive divine power to be more effective in your gardening?

Dig a little deeper:

"Sow with a view to righteousness, reap in accordance with kindness; break up your fallow ground, for it is time to seek the Lord until He comes to rain righteousness on you. You have plowed wickedness, you have reaped injustice, you have eaten the fruit of lies. Because you have trusted in your way..." Hosea 10:12-13a (NAS)

"And He has said to me, My grace is sufficient for you, for power is perfected in weakness. Most gladly, therefore, I will rather boast about my weaknesses, that the power of Christ may dwell in me. Therefore I am well content with weaknesses, with insults, with distresses, with persecutions, with difficulties, for Christ's sake; for when I am weak, then I am strong." 2 Corinthians 12:9-10 (NAS)

Prayer:

God, show me the tools that I need to be effective in my life garden. I confess that I have tried to do things in my own power. I need the power of your Holy Spirit in my life. In Jesus' name, Amen.

Notes:

KEEPING TOOLS HANDY

"My son, do not forget my teaching, but let your heart keep my commandments; for length of days and years of life, and peace they will add to you. Do not let kindness and truth leave you; bind them around your neck, write them on the tablet of your heart. So you will find favor and good repute in the sight of God and man. Trust in the Lord with all your heart, and do not lean on your own understanding. In all your ways acknowledge Him, and He will make your paths straight. Do not be wise in your own eyes; fear the Lord and turn away from evil." Proverbs 3:1-7 (NAS)

It's easy for your tools to get lost while you're working. Several times I laid down my hand clippers and even though they had red handles, I lost them. I might have kicked leaves or dirt onto them. Or as darkness fell, they were in the shadows and I couldn't see them. I learned to keep them very close to me. And even put them in the crook of the tree where I would easily catch sight of them.

I need to be reminded sometimes to keep my spiritual tools close as well. If I haven't spent time in God's Word that day, I will inevitably encounter a problem I'm not ready to handle, especially in the way God desires.

God's Word is so precious. He is gracious and faithful to speak to each one of us through His Word. Whenever I am searching for direction, confirmation, or encouragement in a time of fear or confusion, I can go to His Word. I am thankful that as a child I was encouraged to memorize many scripture passages. It was difficult, but those verses, stored in my memory, are special tools that God can use even when my Bible is not close by.

Have you been faithful to hide God's Word in your heart through memorizing scripture?
Will you make it a priority to use the Master Gardener's Word to sharpen your spiritual tools and keep them close to your heart?

Dig a little deeper:

"Thy word have I hid in mine heart, that I might not sin against thee."
Psalms 119:11 (KJV)

"Remember those who led you, who spoke the word of God to you; and considering the outcome of their life, imitate their faith." Hebrews 13:7 (NAS)

Prayer:

Prayer: Thank you God, that I have your Word and that You speak to me and teach me. Help me to keep it close at all times. In Jesus' name, Amen.

Notes: _____

BLACKBERRIES IN TRAINING

"My prayer for you is that you will overflow more and more with love for others, and at the same time keep on growing in spiritual knowledge and insight, for I want you always to see clearly the difference between right and wrong, and to be inwardly clean, no one being able to criticize you from now until our Lord returns. May you always be doing those good, kind things which show that you are a child of God, for this will bring much praise and glory to the Lord." Philippians 1:9-11 (TLB)

Although blackberry vines are thorny and unfriendly, they bloom with a sweet, soft-pink blossom, and produce berries that taste SO good on vanilla ice cream and in blackberry pie. So I didn't want to do away with all the blackberry vines that crowded our yard.

But in their present condition they were not pleasing to look at, produced few flowers, and thus, only a few berries. Blackberries are much easier to harvest if they are trained to grow in rows. Then you can easily reach both sides of the bushes to pick the berries.

The Bible says that we, as parents, should "train up our children in the way they should go." (Proverbs 22:6) This means in God's way for them, individually, as unique creatures, with His help. Just as I want to train those blackberries to grow a certain way, I want to train my children "to grow in the grace and knowledge of our Lord Jesus Christ." (2 Peter 3:18) I must tend them and care for them. I must encourage them when they are pruned, so they will blossom and bear fruit.

Sometimes God chooses to leave thorns in our lives. He knows He can cause beauty to come from pain in our life and we will eventually produce fruit. Paul asked for the thorn to be removed three times. And God said, "My grace is sufficient for you." (2 Corinthians 12:9) God's grace allowed Paul to bear much fruit despite the thorn.

Have you trained your children to obey God?
Are there thorns in your life God wants to use to help you grow?

Dig a little deeper:

"You did not choose Me, but I chose you, and appointed you, that you should go and bear fruit, and that your fruit should remain; that whatever you ask of the Father in My name, He may give to you." John 15:16 (NAS)

Prayer:

Heavenly Father, give me wisdom and grace in caring for my children and grandchildren. Help me to be sensitive to the way You have made each one of them. In Jesus' name, Amen

Notes: _____

_____

_____

_____

_____

_____

_____

_____

_____

_____

DAY
12

GOOD INTENTIONS

"For I know the plans I have for you,' declares the Lord, 'plans to prosper you and not to harm you, plans to give you hope and a future. Then you will call upon me and come and pray to me, and I will listen to you. You will seek me and find me when you seek me with all your heart. I will be found by you,' declares the Lord." Jeremiah 29:11-14a (NIV)

As blackberry season began in the spring, it became obvious that the bushes I kept were those conveniently located underneath the trees, out of the paths I had created. I soon realized that the berries were getting too much shade and might not ever ripen due to the lack of sun. I hadn't consulted the gardening books and I didn't have all the information I needed when making those decisions.

This has happened often in my life. I intend to do what is right, but sometimes I make decisions without consulting the Master Gardener, or His guidebook, the Bible.

My berries did eventually ripen, although the harvest was affected by my choices. I've decided to allow some of the bushes in the sun to come up from the roots and not mow them off. Next time I'll be more observant of nature before I take things into my own hands.

The choices we make affect the harvest of fruit in our lives as my choice did with the blackberries. A life lived without the Son is a fruitless life. God has a perfect plan for each one of us. And only in knowing and following God's plan will our life bear the most fruit. I have decided to seek God and His Word in each decision I make. The Bible says, "there is a way that seems right to man, but the end thereof is the way of death." Proverbs 14:12 (NAS)

Can you remember a time when your intentions were good, but the decision was not God's best?
How was God faithful to work "all things together for your good"?

Dig a little deeper:

"Whether you turn to the right or to the left, your ears will hear a voice behind you, saying, 'This is the way; walk in it.' He will also send you rain for the seed you sow in the ground, and the food that comes from the land will be rich and plentiful." Isaiah 30:21, 23a (NIV)

Prayer:

God, help me remember to bring every decision to You in prayer. Thank you for turning my good intentions into fruit. Thank you for having a perfect plan for my life. In Jesus' name, Amen.

Notes:

GROWING IN PATIENCE

"For this reason, since the day we heard about you, we have not stopped praying for you and asking God to fill you with the knowledge of his will through all spiritual wisdom and understanding. And we pray this in order that you may live a life worthy of the Lord and may please him in every way: bearing fruit in every good work, growing in the knowledge of God, being strengthened with all power according to his glorious might so that you may have great endurance and patience, and joyfully giving thanks to the Father, who has qualified you to share in the inheritance of the saints in the kingdom of light." Colossians 1:9-12 (NIV)

Waiting for the berries under the trees to ripen took extreme patience. When I failed to see any berries to pick, my first reaction was to loose heart and believe that I had chosen the wrong bushes to leave and that I would never realize my dream of having ripe blackberries. I began to look elsewhere, up and down our street on the empty lots, for other bushes and berries to fulfil my dream. I found many and began an almost daily excursion to pick berries. Occasionally I would go back to the berries in MY yard to check their progress. Finally, the day came when there were ripe berries to pick.

Do you get impatient with some areas of your life? Sometimes it feels like I'm not making the kind of progress I want to make; you know, one step forward and two steps back. And then God reminds me to be patient and to look to Him to bring the maturing and the harvest. He is faithful to send the rain and the sun to the blackberries so that they will grow and mature. Will He not be even more faithful to His children to bring those things into our lives to help us mature and grow?

And how about my impatience with answers to prayer? I was faithful to check for ripe berries even when it seemed there was no progress. Am I as faithful in prayer when there seems to be no change day after day, week after week? Unfortunately, I often give up, or forget to bring the request to God in prayer.

What are you impatient about today?

How have you seen God's faithfulness when you have patiently prayed?

Dig a little deeper:

"How blessed is the man who does not walk in the counsel of the wicked, nor stand in the path of sinners, nor sit in the seat of scoffers! But his delight is in the law of the Lord, and in His law he meditates day and night. And he will be like a tree firmly planted by streams of water which yields its fruit in its season, and its leaf does not wither; and in whatever he does, he prospers." Psalms 1:1-3 (NAS)

Prayer:

God, help me to be patient while you work. Help me to trust in your perfect timing and plan. Thank you for the fruit I see in my life and the lives of those around me. In Jesus name, Amen.

Notes:

GROWING IN HUMILITY

"Come to Me, all who are weary and heavy laden, and I will give you rest. Take My yoke upon you, and learn from Me, for I am gentle and humble in heart; and you shall find rest for your souls. For My yoke is easy, and My load is light." Matthew 11:28-30 (NAS)

Picking blackberries can be backbreaking work. Most of my berries were growing between waist and ankle height. Thus, a lot of bending was required, and breaks were needed to rest my back. Sometimes I would even get dizzy, or lose my balance trying to pick a hard-to-reach berry. After picking for over an hour, I looked up, straightened my back, and I saw some berries at eye level. They were right in front of me. The vines had climbed up into the low branches of a tree and were producing fruit even there.

As we serve God, sometimes we become weary. That's the time to stop, rest, and look up. God brings fruit here, too, when we draw aside, catch our breath, and give thanks.

P.S. All that bending reminded me that I am to humble myself before God, so He can produce fruit in my life. And if I humble myself, He will lift me up.

Do you need to stop and look up?

Have you become weary in your labor for God?

Is your life out of balance?

What has God shown you today that you can thank Him for?

Dig a little deeper:

"This is what the Lord says: 'Stand at the crossroads and look; ask for the ancient paths, ask where the good way is, and walk in it, and you will find rest for your souls.'"Jeremiah 6:16a (NIV)

"Do not be deceived, God cannot be mocked. A man reaps what he sows. The one who sows to please his sinful nature, from that nature will reap destruction; the one who sows to please the Spirit, from the Spirit will reap eternal life. Let us not become weary in doing good, for at the proper time we will reap a harvest if we do not give up." Galatians 6:7-9 (NIV)

Prayer:

God, teach me to walk humbly with You. Lift up my head and my hands when I am weary. Help me to rest in You. In Jesus' name, Amen.

Notes: _____

PLANTED BY GOD

"Fret not yourself because of evildoers, be not envious toward wrongdoers. For they will wither quickly like the grass, and fade like the green herb. Trust in the Lord, and do good; dwell in the land and cultivate faithfulness. Delight yourself in the Lord; and He will give you the desires of your heart. Commit your way to the Lord, trust also in Him, and He will do it." Psalms 37:1-5 (NAS)

At one time I had more than twenty bags of frozen blackberries in my freezer and I had also already given several bags away to friends and family. However, the luscious fruit I was enjoying was not planted by me.

The blackberry bushes on the empty lots were the result of nature and of God. They were a gift from Him. I did not till the ground. I did not plant the bushes. I did not water them. All I did was harvest and enjoy the fruit.

God knows how much I love fresh blackberries and they were His gift to me. Because of this gift I felt accountable to pick them and not to let them wither on the vine. What a waste it would have been to just let them rot. The time that I spent picking them provided a precious time for me to meditate on His Word and for the Master Gardener to teach me some great lessons.

Salvation is a gift. We don't earn it by our actions; we don't deserve it by being good. It is a gift. Our Heavenly Father loves us so much that He sent his Son, Jesus, to die for us, on a cross, so that mankind's relationship with Him could be restored. But, we must accept His gift of salvation. He won't force it on anyone. Just as I accepted responsibility for the blackberries, we must not let His gift of salvation rot on the vine. If we accept it, we will enjoy the sweet relationship and protection He planned for His children.

Have you accepted God's gift of salvation?

What other gifts has God given you that He wants used for His kingdom?

Dig a little deeper:

"Every good and perfect gift is from above, coming down from the Father of the heavenly lights, who does not change like shifting shadows." James 1:17 (NIV)

Prayer:

God, thank you for your precious gift of salvation. You have blessed me with so many gifts. Help me to use those gifts to bring glory and honor to You. In Jesus' name, Amen.

Notes: _____

NO TWO THE SAME

"And He gave some as apostles, and some as prophets, and some as evangelists, and some as pastors and teachers, for the equipping of the saints for the work of service, to the building up of the body of Christ; as a result, we are no longer to be children, tossed here and there by waves, and carried about by every wind of doctrine, by the trickery of men, by craftiness in deceitful scheming; but speaking the truth in love, we are to grow up in all aspects into Him, who is the head, even Christ." Ephesians 4:11-12, 14-15 (NAS)

Blackberries are unique creations. When they begin to form, they are the color of the leaves, therefore hidden and protected. But as they begin to ripen, they turn bright red and contrast beautifully with the green leaves. As the process continues, they turn black and begin to swell. Each tiny bubble of juice catches the light and reflects it. The mature blackberries can be difficult to see in the shadows of the foliage, but when you gently move the leaves aside, the berries reflect the light and we can easily see them.

Some blackberries are showy and grow up high in the direct sunlight. Although easier to see and to find, this makes them susceptible to birds and insects. Other berries grow on or very near to the ground, where they fall prey to rodents and snakes. They are also in danger of mold and heavy rains, which wash them away or cover them with dirt. Then there are the berries that grow in the middle, under the protection of the leaves. When the leaves are moved aside the sun reflects off the juicy orbs, sometimes as big as strawberries. These berries, though easily missed, are usually the biggest, plumpest fruit.

God has created us as individuals. Some of us are showy and rise to the top. Others are content to be hidden in the background. But all of us need God's protection. His love and protection enable us to grow strong and to our full potential. And as we reflect the light from His Son, Jesus, we are fulfilling His command to "let your light shine before men so that they can see your good works and glorify your Father who is in heaven." (Matthew 5:16)

Is there darkness in your life right now?
Are you reflecting the Son?
What has God uniquely created you to do?

Dig a little deeper:

"For you were formerly darkness, but now you are light in the Lord; walk as children of light (for the fruit of the light consists in all goodness and righteousness and truth) trying to learn what is pleasing to the Lord." Ephesians 5:8-10 (NAS)

Prayer:

God, begin today to make me into an oak of Your righteousness for the display of Your splendor. In Jesus' name, Amen.

Notes: _____

DAY
17

STANDING ALONE

"The fruit of the righteous is a tree of life, and he who wins souls is wise." Proverbs 11:30 (NIV)

As I walked up and down the street I was amazed to find here and there a lone blackberry bush. Often it was small and yellowed from the sun and lack of water, easily overlooked among the wildflowers and weeds. But there it was, standing alone, bearing tons of ripe fruit.

Maybe you feel like that lonely blackberry bush at times. Maybe you're a teenager reading this and you feel as if you are the only Christian at your school, in your family, or in your group. Maybe you're an adult in the workplace and there is pressure to just blend in. But you have been called by God to go and bear fruit, to serve your purpose well and make a difference in someone's life.

It made me happy when I would find those single, solitary bushes. And it brings our heavenly Father joy when He sees one of His children standing for Him and standing out for Him. He has called us to be different. And sometimes that may be a lonely feeling. But even though we feel alone, we are never alone. God has promised that "He will never leave us or forsake us." (Hebrews 13:5)

There is a song I love called, Be the One by Al Denson, that says, "Will you be the one to answer to His call? Will you stand when those around you fall? Will you be the one to take His light into a darkened world? Tell me will you be the one?"

Is God calling you to stand alone for Him in your situation?
Will you be the one, or will you blend in with the crowd?
How has God brought fruit into your life as a reward for standing strong for Him?

Dig a little deeper:

"Do you not say, 'Four months more and then the harvest?' I tell you, open your eyes and look at the fields! They are ripe for harvest. Even now the reaper draws his wages, even now he harvests the crop for eternal life, so that the sower and the reaper may be glad together. Thus the saying, 'One sows and another reaps' is true. I sent you to reap what you have not worked for. Others have done the hard work, and you have reaped the benefits of their labor." John 4:35-38 (NIV)

Prayer:

God, help me to stand firm in my faith whatever the consequences. Give me a heart to please You above all others. In Jesus' name, Amen.

Notes:

FOCUSING ON THE PRIZE

"Brethren, I do not regard myself as having laid hold of it yet; but one thing I do; forgetting what lies behind and reaching forward to what lies ahead. I press on toward the goal for the prize of the upward call of God in Christ Jesus." Philippians 3:13-14 (NAS)

As blackberry picking season progressed, I noticed more and more weeds and wildflowers popping up in and around the berry bushes. The berries were still there, but it took more work to move the weeds aside so that I could see what was left to pick. There were some days when I knew there were ripe berries out there needing to be picked, but I just didn't have the energy or the desire to take the time. Sometimes I begged for others to go help with the task. But each time I was faithful, there was a reward waiting for me.

As we journey on through this life there will be times that the weeds of sin and distraction cover up our goals. They draw our time and energy away from God's purpose for our lives, just as the weeds and wildflowers draw water and nutrients away from my blackberry bushes, depriving them of the sun needed for every berry to mature. Therefore, we must keep our focus on Christ and on the prize waiting for us. I desire to hear my Savior say, "Well done, good and faithful servant." (Matthew 25:21)

Have you strayed from or neglected a task God has for you?
Does focusing on the prize make it easier to continue?
What goals have you and God agreed upon?

Dig a little deeper:

"But by the grace of God I am what I am, and His grace toward me did not prove vain; but I labored even more than all of them, yet not I, but the grace of God with me." 1 Corinthians 15:10 (NAS)

"Do you not know that those who run in a race all run, but only one receives the prize? Run in such a way that you may win. And everyone who competes in the games exercises self-control in all things. They then do it to receive a perishable wreath, but we an imperishable. Therefore I run in such a way, as not without aim; I box in such a way, as not beating the air; but I buffet my body and make it my slave, lest possibly, after I have preached to others, I myself should be disqualified." 1 Corinthians 9:24-27 (NAS)

Prayer:

God, help me to keep my eyes on the prize. Help me remember Your goal for me and Christ's example. Help me to finish well. In Jesus' name, Amen.

Notes:

GOD'S BEST

"Therefore, since we have so great a cloud of witnesses surrounding us, let us also lay aside every encumbrance, and the sin which so easily entangles us, and let us run with endurance the race that is set before us, fixing our eyes on Jesus the author and perfecter of faith, who for the joy set before Him endured the cross, despising the shame, and has sat down at the right hand of the throne of God." Hebrews 12:1-2 (NAS)

The most effective picking strategy I've found is to stay in one place and pick every berry I can see and reach from that spot. It always amazes me when I move to the next spot and look back, I see more berries hiding up underneath a leaf or branch. I was standing right in front of them and looking straight down at them, but I could not see them until I moved to a different spot. Then the "hidden" fruit became apparent. Looking back at where I had been, only from a different angle, proved fruitful. Often, I've asked God why a particular thing happened in my life. Sometimes it's only when I look back from a different angle that I see God's hand in that experience and the fruit it produced.

Patience is required to stay and pick in one spot. I saw berries slightly out of my reach and I was tempted to move on and pick the easy ones before finishing the spot I was already in. Satan wants to distract us to move us out of the center of God's will. God's way is the best way. When we deviate from His perfect will, we risk becoming frustrated and missing out on some of the fruit God planned for us.

Do you have a life strategy?
Is it effective? If not, why not?
Are you being patient and waiting for God's best?

Dig a little deeper:

"And the seed in the good ground, these are the ones who have heard the word in an honest and good heart, and hold it fast, and bear fruit with perseverance." Luke 8:15 (NAS)

"Do not fear, for I am with you; do not anxiously look about you, for I am your God. I will strengthen you, surely I will help you, surely, I will uphold you with My righteous right hand." Isaiah 41:10 (NAS)

Prayer:

God, help me not to settle for just the good life. I want Your best. I praise You for giving me the chance to look back and understand some of the whys of my life. Help me to trust You completely when I don't see the fruit. In Jesus' name, Amen.

Notes: _____

_____

_____

_____

_____

_____

_____

_____

_____

THE NEIGHBOR'S VINES

"But I have prayed for you, that your faith may not fail; and you, when once you have turned again, strengthen your brothers." Luke 22:32 (NAS)

On the south edge of our lot there was an old wire fence covered with vines and weeds. I worked hard using wire cutters and pliers to untangle and roll up this broken-down divider. Next, I began to clear out the small saplings and weeds along the property line. Many times the roots of the vines were not even on our lot. The vines had crawled over from the neighbor's lot and climbed around our trees.

Some of the vines had grown to the top of the young trees, and had developed so many leaves, the weight of the vine had bent the trees almost to the ground. As I removed the vines, the trees had to be staked to help them straighten up, or they had to be chopped down.

On one particular tree as the vines grew and climbed around the young trunk, the tree expanded, trying to support the added weight. As the tree matured, the vine cut into the trunk, leaving a rippled effect like a twirly, spiral noodle. It left a permanent scar.

Those we choose to associate with can leave a permanent impression on us. Some leave a good impression and encourage us to walk with God. Others can entangle us in sin, leaving scars for the rest of our lives.

When we are young, or young in our walk with Christ, we must be especially careful about the company we keep. Not that we should exclude non-Christians from our circle of friends, but we must be sure we are strong enough to stand for what is right.

Have others influenced you in a positive way? In a negative way?
When you were a young Christian did something influence you in the wrong way and bring you down?
What helped you overcome this difficulty?

Dig a little deeper:

"Do not be deceived: Bad company corrupts good morals." 1 Corinthians 15:33 (NAS)

"Two are better than one because they have a good return for their labor. For if either of them falls, the one will lift up his companion. But woe to the one who falls when there is not another to lift him up." Ecclesiastes 4:9-10 (NAS)

Prayer:

God, grant me wisdom in choosing my friends. Surround me with others who will help me stand strong for You. Protect me from those who would bring me down. In Jesus' name, Amen.

Notes: _____

PREDATORS

"The Lord is my shepherd; I shall not want. He makes me lie down in green pastures; He leads me beside still waters. He restores my soul; He leads me in the paths of righteousness for His name's sake. Even though I walk through the valley of the shadow of death, I will fear no evil; for Thou art with me; Thy rod and Thy staff, they comfort me. Thou dost prepare a table before me in the presence of my enemies; Thou hast anointed my head with oil; my cup overflows. Surely goodness and mercy will follow me all the days of my life, and I will dwell in the house of the Lord forever." Psalm 23 (NAS)

All varieties of trees and plants are vulnerable to predators such as, vines, insects, fungus, and mold. Moles dig underground and eat the roots. Insects eat the foliage, starving the plant of the nutrients and carbon dioxide it needs to grow. Vines sprout up and strangle trees. There are as many enemies of the plants as there are plants. Yet they survive, and even thrive.

When I first began picking blackberries, it was the moths that were on the bushes chewing away at the fruit. Later the grasshoppers arrived. It reminded me of what Jesus said in Matthew 6:19-21 (NAS) "Do not lay up for yourselves treasures upon earth, where moth and rust destroy, and where thieves break in and steal; but lay up for yourselves treasures in heaven, where neither moth nor rust destroys, and where thieves do not break in or steal; for where your treasure is, there will your heart be also."

Satan has many weapons and the Bible describes him as crafty. He is the deceiver, and camouflages himself when he attacks. Sometimes he attacks and eats away at our family and our faith, our very roots. Often, he uses little things, like jealousy and anger, to eat away at our relationships. And occasionally, he employs drugs and various addictions to achieve a deadly stranglehold.

The good news is that we have a Master Gardener. He tends His garden like a good shepherd tends his sheep. We can trust Him to defeat the predators in our lives. He is our protection, our shield. When we feel vulnerable to Satan's attacks, we can call on God and He will answer. That is His promise. We don't have to be afraid.

What predators do you face?
How has God demonstrated His power to overcome a predator in your life?
Where are you most vulnerable to Satan's attacks?

Dig a little deeper:

"When I am afraid, I will put my trust in Thee." Psalm 56:3 (NAS)

"The Lord lives, and blessed be my rock; and exalted be the God of my salvation, the God who executes vengeance for me, and subdues peoples under me. He delivers me from my enemies; surely Thou dost lift me above those who rise up against me; Thou dost rescue me from the violent man. Therefore I will give thanks to Thee among the nations, O Lord, and I will sing praises to Thy name." Psalm 18:46-49 (NAS)

Prayer:

God, put Your hedge of protection around me. Protect me from the one who seeks to destroy me. In Jesus' name, Amen.

Notes: _____

22

TANGLED FEET

"As for God, his way is perfect; the word of the Lord is flawless. He is a shield for all who take refuge in him. For who is God besides the Lord? And who is the Rock except our God? It is God who arms me with strength and makes my way perfect. You give me your shield of victory; you stoop down to make me great. You broaden the path beneath me, so that my ankles do not turn." 2 Samuel 22:31-33, 36-37 (NIV)

When you're working with vines, it's easy to get your feet tangled. Even when you have just pulled them away from the trees and placed them in a pile, the thorny vines stick to you and your clothes and seem to have a mind of their own. They are especially treacherous when I let down my guard.

I have tripped and fallen many times in my life. It's not fun, and it usually hurts. I tend to look around and see if anyone has seen me fall, embarrassed and humbled.

God's Word says "Pride goes before a fall and a haughty spirit before stumbling." (Proverbs 16:18) When I let down my guard, my pride tends to gets in the way. I'm definitely headed for a tumble. As I look back over some of the most painful experiences of my life, I can see the thorny, sticky vines of pride caused me to be vulnerable.

Just as I must be diligent to see the thorny vines, cut them, and spray them with poison, so also I must daily die to self and ask God to help me keep my pride in check.

Has pride caused you to stumble in the past?
What can you do to keep from being entangled again?

Dig a little deeper:

"God is opposed to the proud, but gives grace to the humble. Submit therefore to God, resist the devil and he will flee from you. Draw near to God and He will draw near to you. Cleanse your hands, you sinners; and purify your hearts, you double-minded. Humble yourselves in the presence of the Lord, and He will exalt you." James 4:6b-8, 10 (NAS)

"My son, let them not depart from your sight; keep sound wisdom and discretion, so they will be life to your soul, and adornment to your neck. Then you will walk in your way securely, and your foot will not stumble. For the Lord will be your confidence and will keep your foot from being caught." Proverbs 3:21-23, 26 (NAS)

Prayer:

God, I confess my pride to You. Give me a humble spirit and keep me from stumbling. In Jesus' name, Amen.

Notes: _____

FALLING DOWN

"For I hope in Thee, O Lord; thou wilt answer, O Lord my God. For I said, 'May they not rejoice over me, who, when my foot slips, would magnify themselves against me.' For I am ready to fall, and my sorrow is continually before me. For I confess my iniquity; I am full of anxiety because of my sin. Do not forsake me, O Lord; O my God, do not be far from me! Make haste to help me, O Lord, my salvation!" Psalm 38:15-18, 21-22 (NAS)

No matter how careful I was when pulling vines out of the ground or pulling down vines entangled in tree branches, sometimes they would give way unexpectedly and I would fall flat. Although I did have a sore wrist from catching myself, and a sore tailbone from a hard landing, I never got seriously hurt. I learned that after falling, it was important to keep moving. Otherwise, when I got home and sat down, my muscles would get stiff and sore.

In my seventy years of life, there have been some falls. I have come away bruised, sometimes embarrassed, and occasionally fearful to get up. And when I fall spiritually, it has been just as important to get up and keep moving forward. If I stop and wallow in self-pity, I'm focusing on myself. But if I look up, and focus on Christ and what He is able to do, I can move forward and learn from my mistakes.

God knows that it's not IF I fall, but WHEN. He's always there to catch me when I fall and set me on my feet again. He soothes the pain and encourages me to try again. I have found the closer I walk with Him, and the more I submit to His will, I seem to have fewer falls.

Have you fallen lately?
Have you reached out to God to help you up?He is waiting to set you on your feet again and heal your pain.

Dig a little deeper:

"It was for freedom that Christ set us free; therefore keep standing firm and do not be subject again to a yoke of slavery." Galatians 5:1 (NAS)

"Be on your guard; stand firm in the faith; be men of courage; be strong. Do everything in love." 1 Corinthians 16:13-14 (NIV)

Prayer:

God, lift me up today. Heal my wounds and set me on my feet again. Strengthen me and help me walk closer to You. In Jesus' name, Amen.

Notes:

WATCH OUT BELOW

*"Gracious is the Lord, and righteous; yes, our God is compassionate.
The Lord preserves the simple; I was brought low, and He saved me.
Return to your rest, O my soul, for the Lord has dealt bountifully with
you. For Thou hast rescued my soul from death, my eyes from tears, my
feet from stumbling. I shall walk before the Lord in the land of the living."*
Psalms 116:5-9 (NAS)

The worst kind of vine has huge thorns, very few leaves and comes straight up from under the ground. It can be as big around as your little finger and as strong as a rope. It will wrap itself around a small tree and completely entangle it. It also climbs up into the tops of taller trees and winds itself around the smaller branches. It seems to seek out and attack the weakest types of trees.

The only way to kill this vine is to cut it off at the root and spray it with poison. Then you must pull the vine out of the tree. Even after being pulled from the tree, these vines are dangerous. It was easy to get my feet caught in them as I continued to work, so I would stomp them down with my shoes as I walked back and forth.

My Savior wore a crown of thorns such as these when he was crucified. They had been woven into a circle and made into something horrible. Jesus wore that crown of thorns and suffered for my sin.

Satan and his armies are wicked. They seek out those who are weak. The only way to overcome them is to allow Christ to cut him off at the root. Jesus now sits on a throne at the Father's right hand and wears a crown of victory. We are assured of this in 1 Corinthians 15:57-58 "But thanks be to God, who gives us the victory through our Lord Jesus Christ. Therefore, my beloved brethren, be steadfast, immovable, always abounding in the work of the Lord, knowing that your toil is not in vain in the Lord." (NAS)

Do you have any areas of weakness that are vulnerable to Satan's attack?

Dig a little deeper:

When I consider Thy heavens, the work of Thy fingers, the moon and the stars, which Thou hast ordained; what is man that Thou dost take thought of him? And the son of man that Thou dost care for him? Yet Thou hast made him a little lower than God, and dost crown him with glory and majesty! Thou dost make him to rule over the works of Thy hands; Thou hast put all things under his feet..." Psalms 8:3-6 (NAS)

"And the God of peace will soon crush Satan under your feet." Romans 16:20 (NAS)

Prayer:

God, help me to be on guard for evil. Protect me from the evil one. Crush him with your mighty power. Holy Spirit, strengthen those areas where I am vulnerable. In Jesus' name, Amen.

Notes: _____

_____

_____

_____

_____

_____

_____

_____

_____

DAY
25

DEADLY DANGER

"But you did not learn Christ in this way, if indeed you have heard Him and have been taught in Him, just as truth is in Jesus, that, in reference to your former manner of life, you lay aside the old self, which is being corrupted in accordance with the lusts of deceit, and that you be renewed in the spirit of your mind, and put on the new self, which in the likeness of God has been created in righteousness and holiness of the truth Be angry, and yet do not sin; do not let the sun go down on your anger, and do not give the devil an opportunity. Let no unwholesome word proceed from your mouth, but only such a word as is good for edification according to the need of the moment, that it may give grace to those who hear. Let all bitterness and wrath and anger and clamour and slander be put away from you, along with all malice. And be kind to one another, tender-hearted, forgiving each other, just as God in Christ also has forgiven you." Ephesians 4:20-27, 29, 31-32 (NAS)

As I was clearing the blackberry thicket, I came across old dead canes among the new blackberry branches. The canes were hard, and the thorns were like sharp needles. They caught on my pants and dug into my skin, even going through my leather gloves. That dead wood is not only dangerous, but it's not healthy for the blackberry bush. It makes the plant susceptible to disease and insects. It also makes it difficult for the blackberries to be harvested.

Sin in our lives, left unconfessed becomes very dangerous. When we harden our hearts and do not allow God to prune out those dead canes it separates us from God and others. The dead wood of unforgiveness in our relationships keeps others at a distance and causes us to be unfruitful, unable to fulfil God's purpose for our life.

But when we confess, and allow God to clean out the dry, dead, dangerous canes of old sins, we are free to get closer to Him. It also allows us to get close to others and share the fruit of the Spirit.

What dead wood does God need to prune from your life?
Is there something or someone you need to forgive?

Dig a little deeper:

"What shall we say then: Are we to continue in sin that grace might increase? May it never be! How shall we who died to sin still live in it. Now if we have died with Christ, we believe that we shall also live with Him, knowing that Christ, having been raised from the dead, is never to die again; death no longer is master over Him. For the death that He died, He died to sin, once for all; but the life that He lives, He lives to God. Even so consider yourselves to be dead to sin, but alive to God in Christ Jesus."
Romans 6:1-11 (NAS)

Prayer:

God, forgive me for my unforgiving heart. Prune out the dead and renew your Spirit in me. In Jesus' name, Amen.

Notes:

DECEIVING APPEARANCES

"Woe to you scribes and Pharisees, hypocrites! For you are like whitewashed tombs, which on the outside appear beautiful, but inside they are full of dead men's bones and all uncleanness. Even so you too outwardly appear righteous to men, but inwardly you are full of hypocrisy and lawlessness." Matthew 23:27-28 (NAS)

Looking back into the corner of our lot you might have seen a nice-looking tree in a small clearing. I had walked through the lot many times and admired this particular tree often. One day, when I got really close, I realized what I thought was a nice, healthy tree, was in fact a dead tree covered with Virginia Creeper vines.

The vines were extremely healthy and had grown up and entangled themselves in the branches of the tree causing its leaves to appear to be the leaves of the tree. Actually, the vines had choked the life from the tree, stolen its nourishment, and blocked the lifegiving sunlight.

I knew the dead tree must be chopped down or during a windstorm it would fall. The vines, you see, were not strong enough to support the tree since the tree had no living roots. When we cut it down, the heart of the tree was rotten. It was completely hollow.

I'm sure that years ago, when the tree was alive, one small vine began to inch its way up the trunk; then two, three, four more followed. No one was around to clear those vines away, so they continued to grow and multiply until it was too late, and the tree died.

Jesus talked about how the Pharisees looked good on the outside but were dead on the inside. Satan would like us to be so caught up in outward appearances, that we neglect our spirit. But God sees deep inside, to the heart. Only when we have true deep roots, can we withstand the storms of life.

Is the health of your spirit a priority? Or are you nurturing your outer appearance and neglecting the nourishment of your soul?
Are you pretending to be something you are not?

Dig a little deeper:

"For the wages of sin is death, but the free gift of God is eternal life in Christ Jesus our Lord." Romans 6:23 (NAS)

"For God so loved the world that He gave His only begotten Son, that whoever believes in Him should not perish, but have eternal life." John 3:16 (NAS)

Prayer:

Dear God, I pray that if there is one person reading this that doesn't know You, they will ask You right now to come into their heart. Father, may they confess their sin, and put their faith in You, Jesus. Help them to sink their roots deep into Your Word and grow in the knowledge and the grace that you will provide. I pray that they will find a church or another Christian that they can share their decision with. In Jesus' name I pray, Amen.

Notes: _____

DAY

27

WEEDY OBSTRUCTIONS

"For we know in part, and we prophesy in part, but when the perfect comes, the partial will be done away. For now we see in a mirror dimly, but then face to face; now I know in part, but then I shall know fully just as I also have been fully known." 1 Corinthians 13:9-10, 12 (NAS)

When we purchased the lot, we couldn't see the boundaries of our property due to overgrown trees and plants. Until some clearing was done there were parts of the lot that we couldn't even walk to. We needed to clear away the weeds and vines obstructing our view in order to see the kinds of trees and bushes that were there.

So it is with our lives. Many things are not clear to us, even when we read God's Word. There have been events in my past that I don't understand and don't know why God allowed them into my life. Sometimes I call out to God for more light to see. And sometimes he answers with more light. Sometimes He reminds me that I have to trust Him.

However, just as I began to see more clearly the good plants and trees on our land, God has been faithful to clear away the scales from my eyes so that I can see where the next step is.

We will not see and understand completely until we are in heaven with Him, but He promises enough light for today. And I trust that He holds my future in His hands and someday, I will see Him clearly, face to face. Then I will not know just the part, but the whole of His plan.

Is there an obstacle keeping you from seeing the path God has for you? Is something keeping you from taking that next step of faith?

Dig a little deeper:

O Lord, Thou has searched me and known me. Thou dost know when I sit down and when I rise up; Thou dost understand my thoughts from afar. Thou dost scrutinize my path and my lying down, and art intimately acquainted with all my ways. Even before there is a word on my tongue, behold, O Lord, Thou dost know it all. Thou hast enclosed me behind and before, and laid Thy hand upon me. Psalm 139:1-5 (NAS)

Prayer:

God, remove anything that is in the way of me seeing clearly what you want from me. Help me trust You and take the next step in faith. In Jesus' name, Amen.

Notes: _____

DAILY MAINTENANCE

"Now for this very reason also, applying all diligence, in your faith supply moral excellence, and in your moral excellence, knowledge; and in your knowledge, self-control, and in your self-control, perseverance, and in your perseverance, godliness; and in your godliness, brotherly kindness, and in your brotherly kindness, Christian love. For if these qualities are yours and are increasing, they render you neither useless nor unfruitful in the true knowledge of our Lord Jesus Christ." 2 Peter 1:5-8 (NAS)

New weeds and vines will grow from old roots and stems. They must continually be cleared out. The longer I keep the areas clean and mulched and spray the vines with weed killer, the easier they are to maintain. Gardening requires perseverance and determination. To me, these are the most frustrating things about gardening and house cleaning. It never stays the same. Something is always moving and changing. I get all the flowerbeds weeded, turn around, and there are more weeds to pull.

I once read a little plaque that said, "Housekeeping is like threading beads on a string with no knot." Just about the time you think you have it all done you must start over again. The same is true of gardening. If I do a little every day it stays fairly clear. If I let it go for a while, I'm in trouble. Maintenance is the key.

In my walk with Christ if I let things go, don't pray, don't read my Bible, then I'm in trouble. If I do a little bit every day, the path stays much clearer. And just as plants mature and grow leaving less space for weeds to take hold, God wants us to be mature "lacking in nothing." (James 1:4) Daily maintenance is the only way to get there. The Christian life takes discipline, perseverance, and determination.

What needs to be a part of your maintenance routine?
Do you need to commit to be more disciplined in your walk with Christ?

Dig a little deeper:

"Since therefore, brethren, we have confidence to enter the holy place by the blood of Jesus, by a new and living way which He inaugurated for us through the veil, that is, His flesh, and since we have a great priest over the house of God, let us draw near with a sincere heart in full assurance of faith, having our hearts sprinkled clean from an evil conscience and our body washed with pure water. Let us hold fast the confession of our hope without wavering, for He who promised is faithful; and let us consider how to stimulate one another to love and good deeds." Hebrews 10:19-24 (NAS)

Prayer:

God, help me to be more disciplined in my daily walk with You. Energize me to do the work you have chosen for me to do. In Jesus' name, Amen.

Notes:

DAY
29

DEATH ON A TREE

"He himself bore our sins in his body on the tree, so that we might die to sins and live for righteousness; by his wounds you have been healed."
I Peter 2:24 (NIV)

Jesus, God's Son, suffered and died on a cross, made by men from one of His creations. His friends anointed his body with herbs and oils taken from plants He created. Then they laid His bloody, beaten, body in a tomb. But on the third day, God raised Jesus from the dead and He lives today in heaven and in our hearts.

The blood I shed when I worked in the trees was nothing compared to the blood He shed for me. It was my sin that put Him on that cross. He willingly sacrificed His life so that I could have eternal life. The Bible says that "without the blood there is no forgiveness of sin." (Hebrews 9:22b) The scars I have and the blood I've shed working out in the trees, are a daily reminder to me of what it cost the Master Gardener to redeem me.

What have we suffered for the cause of Christ?
Have we taken up our cross and followed Him?

Dig a little deeper:

"But if we walk in the light as He Himself is in the light, we have fellowship with one another, and the blood of Jesus His Son cleanses us from all sin. If we say that we have no sin, we are deceiving ourselves, and the truth is not in us. If we confess our sins, He is faithful and righteous to forgive us our sins and to cleanse us from all unrighteousness." 1 John 1:7-9 (NAS)

"And anyone who does not take his cross and follow Me is not worthy of Me. Whoever finds his life will lose it, and whoever loses his life for My sake will find it." Matthew 10:38-39 (NIV)

Prayer:

Jesus, thank you for what You did for me that day on Calvary. Forgive me when I forget about Your pain and suffering. In Your name, Amen.

Notes:

IT IS FINISHED

"For My thoughts are not your thoughts, neither are your ways My ways, declares the Lord. For as the heavens are higher than the earth, so are My ways higher than your ways. For as the rain and the snow come down from heaven, and do not return there without watering the earth, and making it bear and sprout, and furnishing seed to the sower and bread to the eater; so shall My word be which goes forth from My mouth; it shall not return to Me empty, without accomplishing what I desire, and without succeeding in the matter for which I sent it. For you will go out with joy, and be led forth with peace; the mountains and the hills will break forth into shouts of joy before you, and all the trees of the field will clap their hands, instead of the thorn bush the cypress will come up; and instead of the nettle the myrtle will come up; and it will be a memorial to the Lord, for an everlasting sign which will not be cut off." Isaiah 55:8-13 (NAS)

Gardening, like life, is an ongoing process. There is the planting season, harvesting season, ground preparation, fertilization, and the constant maintenance. But if we finish the tasks required in a garden, we will experience the joy and the fruit of our labor, whether in real fruit, or in beautiful flowers and trees.

I pray each year of my life will be more beautiful to my heavenly Father than the one before. As I finish this task of recording all He has taught me in my garden, I sing this song to God:

"It's been such a hard year, I don't understand.
Seems like nothin's gone my way.

I try to spend time with the ones I love.
I wish there were more hours in a day.

And it feels like I'm moving way to fast, I've been running far too long.
I want to get back to my first love and be where I belong.
There's a place I can go where I know You'll be;
I just close my eyes and let Your love take hold of me.

So come meet me Father, at my home with a view.
Where I can look out on the water and spend time with you.
I won't worry about tomorrow, you will see me through.
So come meet me Father, at my home with a view.

The sun shines on the water, to make a stained-glass sea.
A songbird on the rooftop, singing perfectly.
It all started on a hillside, with Your Son upon a tree.
I believe He died and rose again and that's why He's here with me.

So come meet me Father, at my home with a view.
Where I can look out on the water and spend time with you.
I won't worry about tomorrow, you will see me through.
So come meet me Father, at my home with a view."

"Home With a View" by John Elefante
Defying Gravity

Dig a little deeper:

"I have brought you glory on earth by completing the work you gave me to do. And now, Father, glorify me in your presence with the glory I had with you before the world began." John 17:4-5 (NIV)

Prayer:

Jesus, help me to follow Your example and complete the work God has for me in this life, for Your glory. In Jesus name, Amen.

DAY
31

THE PERFECT GARDEN

"Rejoice in the Lord always; again I will say, rejoice! Let your forbearing spirit be known to all men. The Lord is near. Be anxious for nothing, but in everything by prayer and supplication with thanksgiving let your requests be made known to God. And the peace of God, which surpasses all comprehension, shall guard your hearts and your minds in Christ Jesus. Finally, brethren, whatever is true, whatever is honorable, whatever is right, whatever is pure, whatever is lovely, whatever is of good repute, if there is any excellence and if anything worthy of praise, let your mind dwell on these things. Philippians 4:4-8 (NAS")

That place where the garden always stays perfect is a reality. It's called heaven. There will be no thorns, weeds, or thorny vines there, only beauty. What a view that home will have! I can't wait to get there and start gardening.

Until then, I'll continue to work in the garden he has given me now. I will enjoy and be thankful for each day that I get to spend in His creation. I will try to pass on what I know and what He has taught me about life and gardening to my children, grandchildren, friends and family until He comes to take me home.

What do you think of when you think of heaven?

Dig a little deeper:

"Behold, I will create new heavens and a new earth. The former things will not be remembered, nor will they come to mind. But be glad and rejoice forever in what I will create, for I will create Jerusalem to be a delight and its people a joy. I will rejoice over Jerusalem, and take delight in my people; the sound of weeping and of crying will be heard in it no more. Never again will there be in it an infant who lives but a few days, or an old man who does not live out his years; he who dies at a hundred will be thought a mere youth; he who fails to reach a hundred will be considered accursed. They will build houses and dwell in them; they will plant vineyards and eat their fruit. No longer will they build houses and others live in them or plant and others eat. For as the days of a tree, so will be the days of my people; my chosen ones will long enjoy the works of their hands. They will not toil in vain or bear children doomed to misfortune; for they will be a people blessed by the Lord, they and their descendants with them. Before they call I will answer; while they are still speaking I will hear. The wolf and the lamb will feed together, and the lion will eat straw like the ox, but dust will be the serpent's food. They will neither harm nor destroy on all my holy mountain, says the Lord." Isaiah 65:17-25 (NIV)

"Do not let your hearts be troubled. Trust in God; trust also in me. In my Father's house are many rooms, if it were not so, I would have told you. I am going there to prepare a place for you. And if I go and prepare a place for you, I will come back and take you to be with me that you also may be where I am." John 14:1-3 (NIV)

Prayer:

God, help me to fix my eyes on things above. Help me to not expect perfection of myself or others here. But help me to eagerly wait for your return for me. In Jesus' name, Amen.

Notes: _____

_____

_____

_____

_____

_____

_____

Author

Anita Wadley Schlaht

Anita Edwards Wadley Schlaht was born in Kansas City, Missouri. She and her family moved from Neosho, Missouri to Edmond, Oklahoma in 1960. At the age of seven Anita began her walk with Jesus and found that while she spent quiet times among the trees at GA Camp, He was speaking through His Word about the direction for her life. One of her life verses is Galations 2:20, "I am crucified with Christ, nevertheless I live, yet not I but Christ liveth within me. And the life which I now live in the flesh, I live by the faith in the Son of God, who loved me and gave Himself for me."

Anita remembers visiting her maternal grandmother and spending time in the garden with her. Blanche loved flowers and grew all kinds of vegetables in the summertime. Anita remembers picking pears and wrapping them in newspaper to store in the cellar, picking up pecans from her trees, learning to can tomatoes and beans, and picking flowers for a table bouquet. Anita's grandmother was a godly woman who studied her Bible and knelt beside the bed to pray each night.

Schlaht graduated high school in 1971, college in 1974, and received her M.Ed. in Gifted Education in 1992. She owned and ran her own preschool for 25 years and taught kindergarten in the Edmond Public Schools for four years. She remembers a poem from those years that ends, "I love to work in the garden where little children grow."

Anita wrote the internationally known poem "Just Playing" in 1974. It was published in calendars, booklets, posters, curriculum guides, Chicken Soup for the Unsinkable Soul, and as a children's book in 2018. She published three short stories in the Guidepost's "When Miracles Happen" series in 2007 and 2008.

Anita retired in 2019 after five years as Executive Director of the Edmond Historical Society and Museum. She is passionate about studying God's Word and has been drawn to the missions' ministries at Henderson Hills Baptist Church in Edmond where she uses her gifts of teaching, writing, music, sewing and crochet.

Anita and her husband Kirby have a blended family of six children and nine grandchildren. They enjoy their membership together in the Edmond Iris and Garden Society, travelling and visiting botanical gardens wherever they go, reading, sports, and music.

CPSIA information can be obtained
at www.ICGtesting.com
Printed in the USA
JSHW011210120323
38764JS00003B/135